4/04

KIDS & COMPUTERS

Kids & Computers

The Minicomputers

Charles A. Jortberg

Published by Abdo & Daughters, 4940 Viking Drive, Suite 622, Edina, Minnesota 55435.

Copyright © 1997 by Abdo Consulting Group, Inc., Pentagon Tower, P.O. Box 36036, Minneapolis, Minnesota 55435 USA. International copyrights reserved in all countries. No part of this book may be reproduced in any form without written permission from the publisher.

Printed in the United States.

Cover and Interior Photo credits: Wide World Photos
Archive Photos
Jortberg Associates

Edited by John Hamilton

Library of Congress Cataloging-in-Publication Data

Jortberg, Charles A.
   The minicomputers / Charles A. Jortberg.
    p. cm. -- (Kids and computers)
   Includes index.
   Summary: Describes the development of minicomputers, how they work, and how they are used.
   ISBN 1-56239-726-5
   1. minicomputers--Juvenile literature. [1. minicomputers. 2. Computers] I. Title. II. Series: Jortberg, Charles A. Kids and computers.
QA76.52.J675 1997
004.16'09--DC20

                        96-28296
                        CIP
                        AC

About the Author

Charles A. Jortberg graduated from Bowdoin College in 1951 with a Bachelor's Degree in Economics. Mr. Jortberg joined IBM in 1954 and served in several capacities. Among his assignments were coordinating all of IBM's efforts with the Air Force, managing a 20-person team of IBM engineers, and directing a number of technical programs at NASA's Electronic Research Laboratory. He formed Jortberg Associates in 1972, where he currently works, to provide an outlet for his start-up technology experience.

Contents

The Mini Revolution

As minicomputers became popular, thousands of new computer installations took place around the world. There seemed to be no limit to the new uses for these machines. As minicomputers found many new challenges in solving problems, there were developments in the electronics industry that would change the world of computers. These developments, which started in the 1960s and continue today, allowed for a major reduction in size of the electronic components used in computers.

These new developments allowed computers the size of a postage stamp to be built. Although these new machines are very small, they are hundreds of times more powerful than the original big machines. This great increase in power has been made possible at a fraction of the price of the original computers. Today you can buy 600 computers for the price of one of the old slower machines.

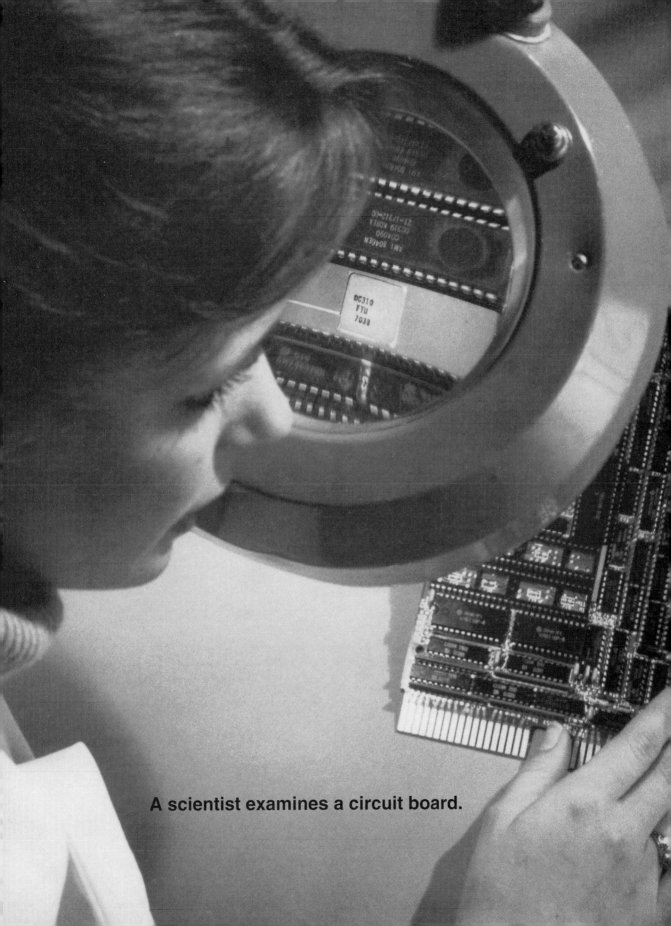

A scientist examines a circuit board.

The Transistor

The revolution in miniaturization goes back to a man named Jack Kilby, who invented the transistor in 1948. This important invention allows electronic devices to be built that take up much less room, require less electricity, and are hundreds of times faster than the older computers.

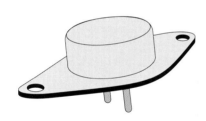

A transistor.

Major breakthroughs still continue in this field of electronics, which is called the semiconductor industry. These inventions include a lot of different electronic parts that continue to reduce the size of computers and at the same time speed them up. When the transistor was invented, it could do the same thing as a bulky switch in the old machines. The transistor was only the size of an eraser on a pencil, while the switch could be over a foot long. This reduction in size still continues today. It is now possible to build a million of these transistors in a square that is not as big as the same eraser.

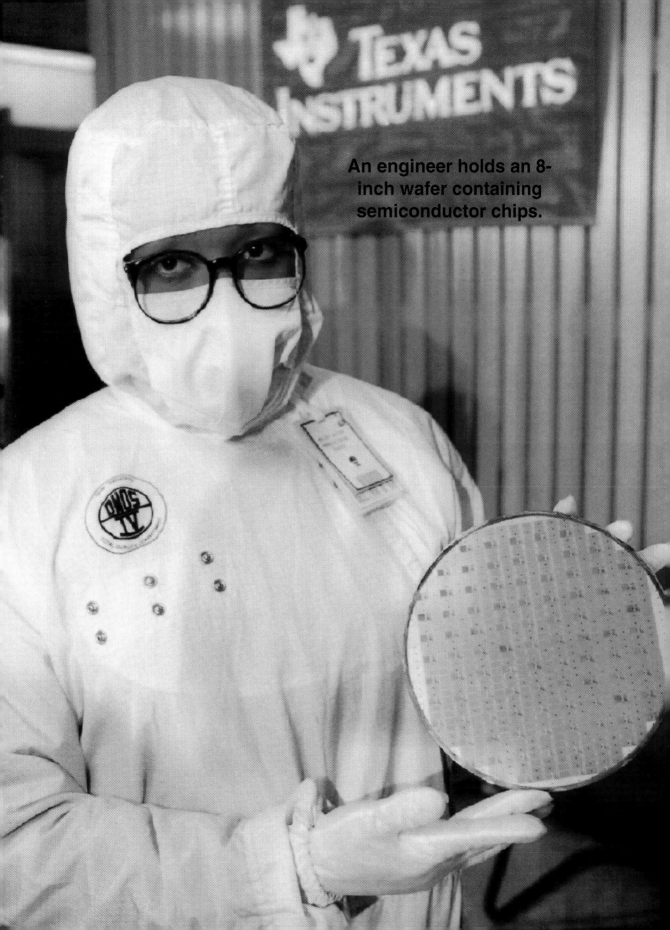

An engineer holds an 8-inch wafer containing semiconductor chips.

The electrical circuits for these miniatures are first laid out in a drawing, with each line representing a wire. In some cases the picture can be as big as a wall. These big pictures have hundreds of lines. A special camera is then used to take a photograph of the big picture. This picture is then shrunk in size until each line is only 1/100th the size of a human hair.

The tiny picture is treated with special chemicals and then baked in a high-temperature oven. Tiny transistors are actually "grown" in just the right places as each of the lines become hair-like wires. This process produces a "chip." These wires and transistors are so small that if a speck of dirt lands on the material it ruins the chip.

To guard against dirt, chips are made in special areas called "clean rooms." The air in these rooms is put through special equipment to remove all dirt. The air in clean rooms contain no pieces of dust bigger than one millionth of an inch.

People who work in clean rooms wear special white clothing that covers every inch of their bodies. Even their shoes have special covers so that they don't track anything into the room. When the workers check the chips to be sure they are built correctly, they work with special microscopes that enlarge the hair-like wires.

Chips are used in several parts of today's computers. In the early 1970s engineers were able to design one of these chips that contained all of the elements of a big computer.

This reduction in size meant that a big computer needing a separate room in the 1950s could now be put on a chip the size of an eraser. This new invention was called a "microprocessor." Even though the microprocessor was contained on a chip, it had the same elements as the bigger computers. Other small chips contained the memory needed for the computer.

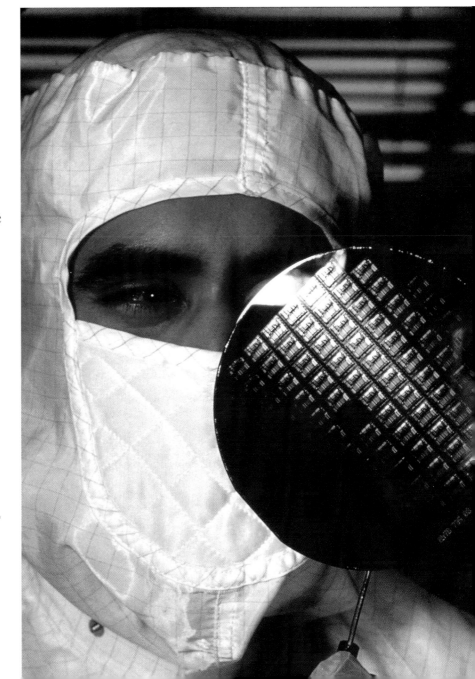

A wafer full of 32-bit superchips.

The Micro-processor

The microprocessor is now used in many of the things we use every day. There are microprocessors in our cameras to sense the light and set the lens for perfectly exposed and focused pictures. Microprocessors in our cars automatically check how various parts are working and let us know when there is a problem. In our televisions, these processors keep track of what channels we like to watch, and keep the picture focused.

A microprocessor.

Many of our wristwatches now contain microprocessors that keep accurate time or sound an alarm. Video games have at least one microprocessor, and some have two or three. There are few places in our daily life where we don't have some contact with microprocessors.

A hand-held computer designed with the use of microprocessors.

Personal Computers

One of the most important inventions made possible by the microprocessor was the personal computer. These computers, called "PCs," have greatly affected our lives in our homes, our schools, our work, and our play.

The first PCs were actually kits that you could buy in stores. When you brought the kit home and assembled it, you could attach it to your TV to display your information. The retail chain Radio Shack offered a PC that could use standard music cassettes to store data in the same way that the big tape units were used with the larger machines.

In the late 1970s two young men from California started to experiment with microprocessors in their garage. They invented the first machine that began the personal computer revolution. Stephen Wozniak and Steve Jobs used their invention to launch a company called Apple Computer. The Apple computer was the first PC designed for easy use. The machine also had an affordable price.

Apple cofounders Steve Jobs (left) and Stephen Wozniak (right) unveil the Apple IIc.

The Apple computer was the first machine to use a "mouse." Created by Douglas Englebart, the mouse helped people communicate with their computers. Many of the computer displays had small pointers that showed which information in the computer you were working with at any time. These pointers are called "cursors." By moving the cursor, you can also direct the computer where you want to go next.

A computer with a mouse (lower right).

Before the mouse was invented, you had to move the cursor by hitting several computer keys. This took a long time if you were on the top line of the display and you wanted the cursor on the bottom line. The mouse is wired so that the cursor is controlled by the mouse movements. By putting the mouse on a flat surface next to the computer and moving it, the cursor on the screen moves the same direction, as if you were pointing at the cursor and moving it. If you want to move from one line to another point 20 lines away, you merely move the mouse down until the cursor stops at the desired point.

In the Apple computer, the mouse was used for many tasks. The computer used pictures of things on the screen for easy and faster use. These pictures are called "icons," and are widely used today in most PCs.

Using the mouse, you position the cursor over an icon representing something you want to do. For example, if you want to delete a date file, you click on the file and then drag it over an icon that looks like a trash can.

The popularity of the Apple computer surprised many in the computer industry. Soon thousands of units had been sold, many to colleges and high schools to teach students the power of computing. The PC became so powerful and so common that today nearly every college requires students to have a computer.

An icon (upper right) representing the computer's hard drive.

After other computer companies saw how popular the Apple computer had become, they all jumped in. IBM was one of the last companies to develop a PC. They didn't want to replace their big machines with the smaller, less expensive computers. But once IBM began to sell its PC, the machine quickly became very popular. Demand was so high that many new companies were formed to sell computers that were copies of IBM's PC. Called "clones," most of these copies were less expensive and worked just as well.

The Semi-conductor

As PCs became more and more popular, many companies in the semiconductor industry rushed to make computer chips smaller and more powerful. These companies also made memory chips that could store millions of numbers or letters. In addition to these chips, a new group of memory products were being developed that allowed more storage than ever before possible.

Companies in California invented a new kind of disk memory that stored millions and millions of bits of data for use in small computers. These disks were small units, about the size of a three-ring notebook. Each disk unit contained from two to six disks that looked like records stacked on a stereo. These units, known as "hard disk drives," could store millions of numbers and letters that could be used by the computer. The information on these disks is read into the computer by an arm that moves in and out to the location of the data you want.

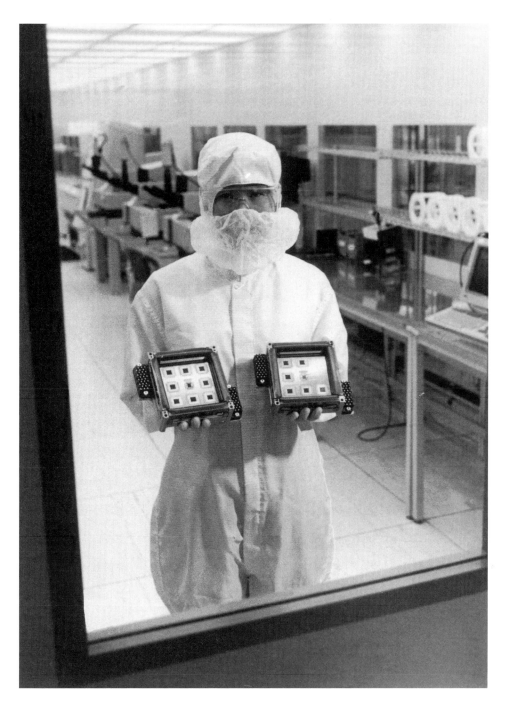

An engineer displays multi-semiconductor chip units that will be used in mainframe computers.

Hard disks are located inside the case of the computer, and stay there with information being moved to and from the computer. Other disks were developed that allow you to bring information in and out of the machines by having portable "floppy disks." The name came from the first ones developed, which were five and one quarter inches square and were very flexible. The newer disks are rigid and are only three and one half inches square. Each of these smaller disks can store more than two and one half million numbers or letters.

Portable floppy disks can be used to store information outside the computer. When you have important files, it's a good idea to "back up" the files by having copies outside the machine. If your computer fails, you can then read the files back in from the disks. Other backup systems include tape cassettes, removable hard drives, and optical drives.

Opposite Page: A masked technician catches his reflection on the polished surface of a data storage disk.

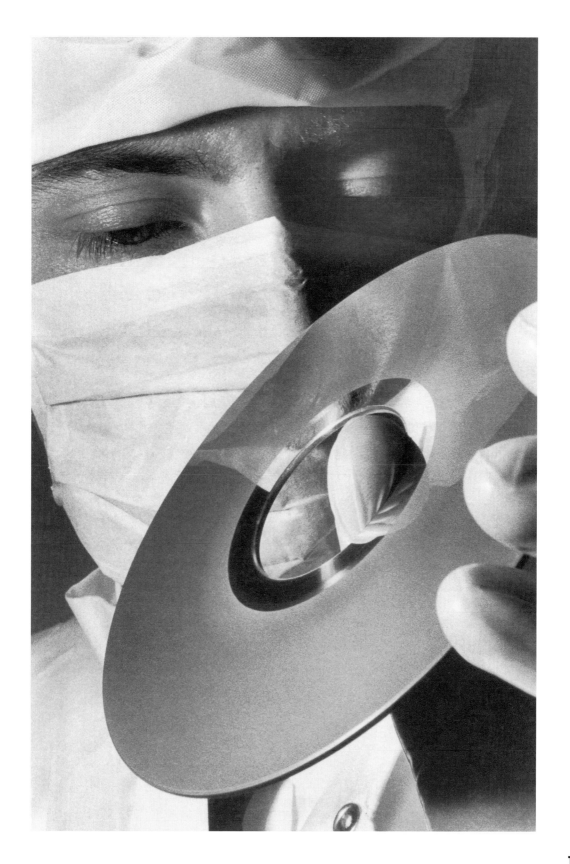

CD-ROM

Many PCs now use another kind of disk that is very popular for recorded music. The compact disk, or CD, is now widely used for storing big volumes of data that computers often use. Since the information can only be read from these disks, they are called CD-ROM. This term comes from the first letters of the term "Compact Disk Read Only Memory." These disks are recorded at a studio or a factory and the information is permanently stored on the disk.

The CD-ROM's information is recorded with a laser beam. The laser burns tiny holes on the surface of the disk, with the pattern of the holes representing bits of data. One big advantage of a CD-ROM is the large amount of data that can be stored. Entire encyclopedias can be stored on one CD-ROM. Other uses include large data bases, such as telephone listings, or multimedia games that require huge graphics files.

**The compact disk is lightweight and one-sixth
the size of old records.**

Communications

Pcs can communicate with a number of locations by using a device called a "modem." A modem connects the computer to telephone lines, translates thousands of numbers and letters per second into sound signals, then sends the signals through the lines. At the receiving end, another computer with a modem changes the signals back to the digital impulses the computer uses.

PCs can communicate with each other without using telephone lines. These computers are connected in a system known as a "Local Area Network," or LAN. In a LAN, one computer controls the movement of data from one computer to another to be sure that nothing is lost. This unit is known as the "server." In some LANs, computers outside the same location can also join in by using telephone lines and modems.

As computers, including PCs, became complex, it was important to program them easily and to take advantage of all

Opposite page: A portable personal computer which uses a modem to transmit documents via radio waves.

the features built into them. Programming languages like FORTRAN and COBOL were developed to allow users to write programs in terms people are used to. FORTRAN stands for Formula Translator, and is used to write programs for mathematical problems. COBOL stands for Common Business Oriented Language, and is used for business-type problems. A number of other programming languages are designed to make it easy to use computers.

As the PC became widely used, almost all of the things needed to run a business had programs written to install them easily on a small computer. The word processing users changed from minicomputers to PCs, and all the accounting records were easily transferred. Many tasks performed on the big machines were now being done on faster and better PCs.

One of the best uses of a PC and a LAN is in systems that join a number of computers together by communication lines into groups. These groups are usually people who are working together, and the computers are used constantly to exchange information from computer to computer.

If everyone in your classroom had a computer and they were connected by communication lines, each student could write a page of a report and it would be available for everyone to see on their displays. If you had a system like this, the teacher could leave homework assignments on the computer and you could display them at any time. You could even call from home and find out what homework is due for next week!

A new line of IBM personal computers being displayed.

The Operating System

With all the features, devices, and programming languages in computers, it's important to keep track of everything and to be sure all the pieces are in place. A master program called an "operating system" is used by many computers for this control. In the world of personal computers, the operating system most often used is "Windows," which is sold by Microsoft. When the latest version of Windows (Windows 95) was released, over one million copies were sold the first week. The young man who started Microsoft, Bill Gates, is now the richest person in the United States.

The microprocessor has become so small and powerful that new computers are now being made that are the size of three-ring notebooks. These miniature systems are just as powerful as

Bill Gates,
Chairman of
Microsoft
Corporation.

most full-size systems. These computers are called "laptops," since you can put the computer on your lap.

These little machines have as much memory as the big machines. The internal memory can store hundreds of thousands of numbers and letters, and the hard disks can store millions. The display screen is part of the outer cover. When you open it, the display is right there. Some laptops have full-color displays, while others use black and white.

Some laptops use a separate mouse, which is stored in the case when not in use. Others use a small button that is part of the keyboard. Pressing this button one way or the other moves the cursor just like a mouse. Other laptops use a "track ball." This looks like a ball that is contained in a case, with only the top of the ball showing. When the ball is rolled one way or another, the cursor on the screen moves the same way. Many video games use these same types of devices.

As the rush to make computers smaller continues, there are now PCs called "palmtops." These units are so small they fit in a shirt pocket. Although their memory is somewhat smaller, these units are nearly equal to the full-sized PC that needs a desk. Palmtops are about the size of a small hand-held video game. Many of these video games contain the same type of microprocessors as the PC.

Some people don't like laptop and palmtop computers because of the smaller keyboards. The keys are so small that many times you hit two at once by mistake. There are now systems where a full-size keyboard folds up in the case when not in use and opens up when you open the case.

A laptop computer.

Voice Systems

For many years, computer scientists have been trying to build a computer that understands the human voice. They have finally made it happen with systems that work with the PC. When you speak into a microphone, electrical signals are created that the computer converts into numbers.

When you first start with a voice system, you speak certain words into the microphone and the system "learns" how you speak. This learning period is needed because people from different parts of the country sound different.

After this learning period you can keep dictating words you use a lot and the computer stores them in memory in a file with your name on it. After you have built up the vocabulary you can just tell the computer your name and start talking. The computer goes to your memory area and finds the words you are speaking.

After the words are found, they are put into memory and you can do anything you want with them, such as word processing. Other voice systems are used to give orders to the computer. In a hospital operating room, doctors and nurses have their hands full and can't use a mouse to move a cursor on a computer showing an X ray or test results. By speaking a command they can move the cursor up, down, or sideways.

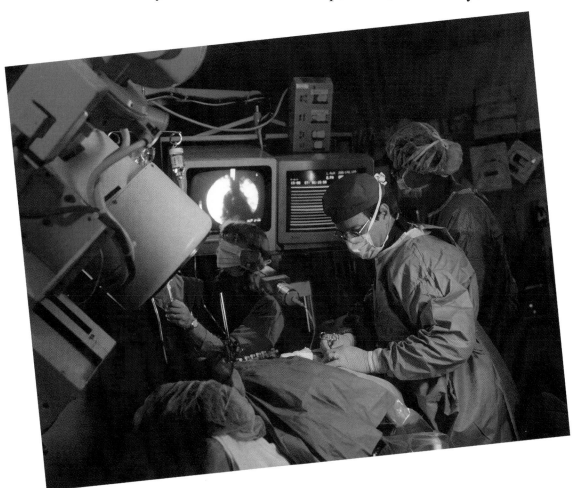

Doctors using computers in the operating room.

Other Micro- processor Uses

Cameras

Several camera companies have developed digital cameras that store photographs as a series of numbers on a disk instead of recording on film. These numbers can then be transferred to a PC, which displays the picture on a screen. If you like the picture, you can save it on disk, or print a copy.

Supercomputers

While the microprocessor has come to mean a very small but powerful computer on a chip, it is also part of the most powerful computers in the world. These machines are known as "supercomputers," and they operate at blinding speed. Many of these machines can do over a million math problems per second.

Supercomputers are built by taking thousands of very small microprocessors and wiring them together in giant machine. When a very difficult problem needs to be solved, some of the processors work on one part of the problem, while other processors work on another part. When all the parts are finished, there is one place where the answer is stored. This process of using more than one processor in a computer system at the same time is called "parallel processing."

Supercomputers are used for solving some very big problems. They help develop weather maps for the whole world. Future space flights are also being planned with every detail of the mission worked out beforehand. These supercomputers are even developing pictures on their screens that show what the climate conditions are on the surfaces of Mars, Jupiter, and other planets.

Medical Uses

The microprocessor is used in many areas of medicine. There are many things now being done that were impossible before the microprocessor. In the operating room doctors can use lasers controlled with microprocessors. In patients' rooms complex instruments—all with microprocessors—keep close track of heartbeats and blood pressure.

One of the most exciting uses of microprocessors is in the treatment of people who have been paralyzed by automobile, diving, or other accidents. Many of these people can't walk because their spinal cords have been damaged.

The spinal cord is like a big cable that carries instructions from the brain, in the form of electrical signals, to every part of the body. When the spinal cord is injured, the signals from the brain can't get through, and the injured person often loses the use of their legs. Doctors are developing computer programs that will take the place of the spinal column and send signals to the legs. They have made this work in several cases using a larger computer. These doctors are now developing a microprocessor that will do the same thing and be carried in the patient's pocket.

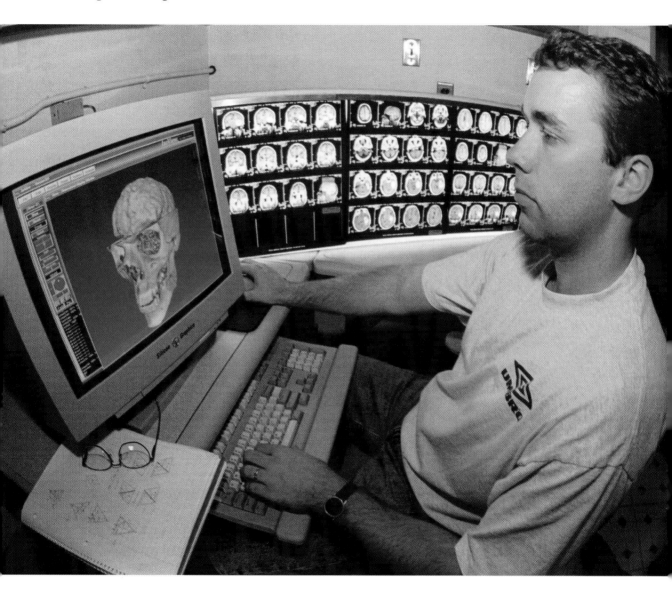

A medical student works on a program called "Iso View" which gives doctors a three-dimensional view of a person's head, neck, and shoulders.

Glossary

BASIC - Beginners All-Purpose Symbolic Instruction Code; a simple programming language.

CD-ROM - Compact disk—Read Only Memory. A disk that stores data and instructions which can be retrieved and used but never altered.

check sorting machine - Machines used by banks to read special coded account numbers, and to sort checks by account numbers.

circuit - An electronic device containing thousands of electrical components combined on one chip.

clone - Any of a group of identically reproduced computers.

COBOL - Common Business Oriented Language. A program language used for business-type problems.

compiler - Program that translates instructions.

control panels - Place where instructions were wired to solve problems.

cursor - A small pointer that shows which information in the computer you are working with at any time.

data - A collection of information.

digital - Having to do with a system of numbers, particularly the digits 0 and 1, that are stored in a computer and represent data or information.

floppy disk - A thin, flexible disk that stores data in the form of magnetic patterns on its surface.

FORTRAN - A special compiler for scientific work (Formula Translation).

graphic - Paintings, photography, and other art in which forms are represented visually.

hard disk drive - A device that rotates a magnetic storage disk and that can record and retrieve data.

icon - A graphic symbol.

laboratory instrument computer (LINC) - Small scientific computer used for experiments in hospitals and laboratory tests.

LAN - A system known as a "Local Area Network" that links a series of computers.

laptop - A flat, portable, minicomputer that can fit on a person's lap.

laser - A device that produces an extremely powerful beam of light.

laser printer - A printer that uses laser beams to "burn" letters, characters, and images onto paper.

microprocessor - A single chip containing all the components found in the computer's central processing unit.

modem (*mo*dulator *dem*odulator) - An input-output device that translates a computer's digital pulses into sound for transmission over telephone lines or other communication networks to another computer.

mouse - A device used to move a computer's cursor.

multimedia - Something that uses a variety of media, including graphics, sound, text, and motion pictures.

operating system - A linked series of programs that control all other programs on the computer.

optical drive - A nonmetallic external storage device.

palmtop - A small, flat, portable computer that fits in the palm of the hand.

PC - Personal computer; an affordable desktop computer designed specially for personal use.

program - A step-by-step series of instructions directing the computer to carry out a sequence of actions in order to perform an operation or to solve a problem.

SABRE - A reservation-handling machine built for American Airlines by IBM.

semiconductor chip - A thin slice of silicon containing an integrated circuit.

supercomputer - A computer with thousands of very small microprocessors that can do over a million math problems per second.

timesharing - The sharing of one large computer by several users. Users were connected by telephone lines to the central machine.

transistor - A very small electronic device containing semiconductors which are used to control the strength of electric currents.

word processing - The most common use of the minicomputer; used in offices to write letters, edit documents and perform record keeping.

Index

K

keyboard 28, 29
Kilby, Jack 6

L

laptops 28, 29
lasers 20, 34
lens 10
Local Area Network (LAN) 22, 24,
    37

M

Mars 33
medicine 34
memory 9, 16, 20, 28, 30
micorphone 30
microprocessor 9, 10, 12, 26, 28,
    32, 33, 34, 35, 38
Microsoft 26
miniaturization 6, 8, 26
modems 22
mouse 14, 15, 28, 31
multimedia 20
music cassettes 12

O

operating room 31, 34
operating system 26
optical drive 1 8

P

palmtops 28, 29
parallel processing 33
personal computers 12, 14, 15, 16,
    20, 22, 23, 24, 26, 28, 30, 32

photographs 32
programming 23, 24, 26

R

Radio Shack 12
removable hard drive 18

S

school 12, 15
scientists 30
semiconductors 6, 16
server 22
sound signals 22
space flight 33
stereo 16
students 15
supercomputers 33

T

tape cassettes 18
telephone 22
television 10
track ball 28
transistor 6, 8

V

video games 10, 28

W

windows 26
word processing 31
Wozniak, Stephen 12
wristwatch 10

V

X ray 31